This book belongs to:

_____

One Creator
Many Names

Qur'an Shakir

One Creator, Many Names
Qur'an Shakir
illustrations by Qur'an Shakir
& Microsoft Bing Image Creator

ISBN: 978-1-966132-07-3
Published by B.U.B.I
(Building Us Beyond Imagination) Publishing
November 2025
Atlanta, Georgia
United States of America, USA

Copyrighted 2025
All rights reserved. No part of this book may be reproduced or used in any manner without the prior written permission of the copyright owner, except for the use of brief quotations in a book review.

Disclaimer

Handle with Care

Because this book contains some of the sacred words from revelation, We kindly ask that you consciously take good care of this book. Do not sit it in dirty places or leave it in places known as impure.

This book is a love offering in honor of The One, The Almighty, by whatever name one may call Him. Every effort has been made to present the words, teachings, and visuals with care and accuracy. If there are any errors or oversights, please forgive us. The errors were never our intention.

Thank you for your mercy, understanding, and grace.

This book was created to celebrate the beauty of our shared faith in The One — by whatever name we call Him. Through years of interfaith work, I've seen how prayer, compassion, and understanding unite us more deeply than our differences divide us.

May this book help children, and all of us, remember that we are one human family, created by One Divine Designer.

— Madame Q

Dedication

To all children of the world, may you grow in wonder, kindness, and love for every creature, and may you always know that every prayer is heard.

بِسْمِ اللَّهِ الرَّحْمَنِ الرَّحِيْمِ

Some call
The Creator Allah

(Qur'an 2:186).

Some say Lord, God

(Bible, Matthew 6:9).

Others whisper
Yahweh, Elohim, Adonai

(Torah, Deuteronomy 6:4).

Some say,
"Oh, Great Spirit"

Some bow saying The
Beneficent, The Merciful

(Qur' an 1:1).

Some say The Almighty,
The One, so powerful.

(Bible, Revelation 15:3)

Love the Lord Your God

The Qur'an says:
"Call on Allah, or call on The Beneficent.
By whatever name you call Him,
He has the Most Beautiful Names."
(Qur'an 7:180)

The Prophet Muhammed, peace be upon him, prayed:
"O Allah, I call on You by every name You have."
(Musnad Ahmad)

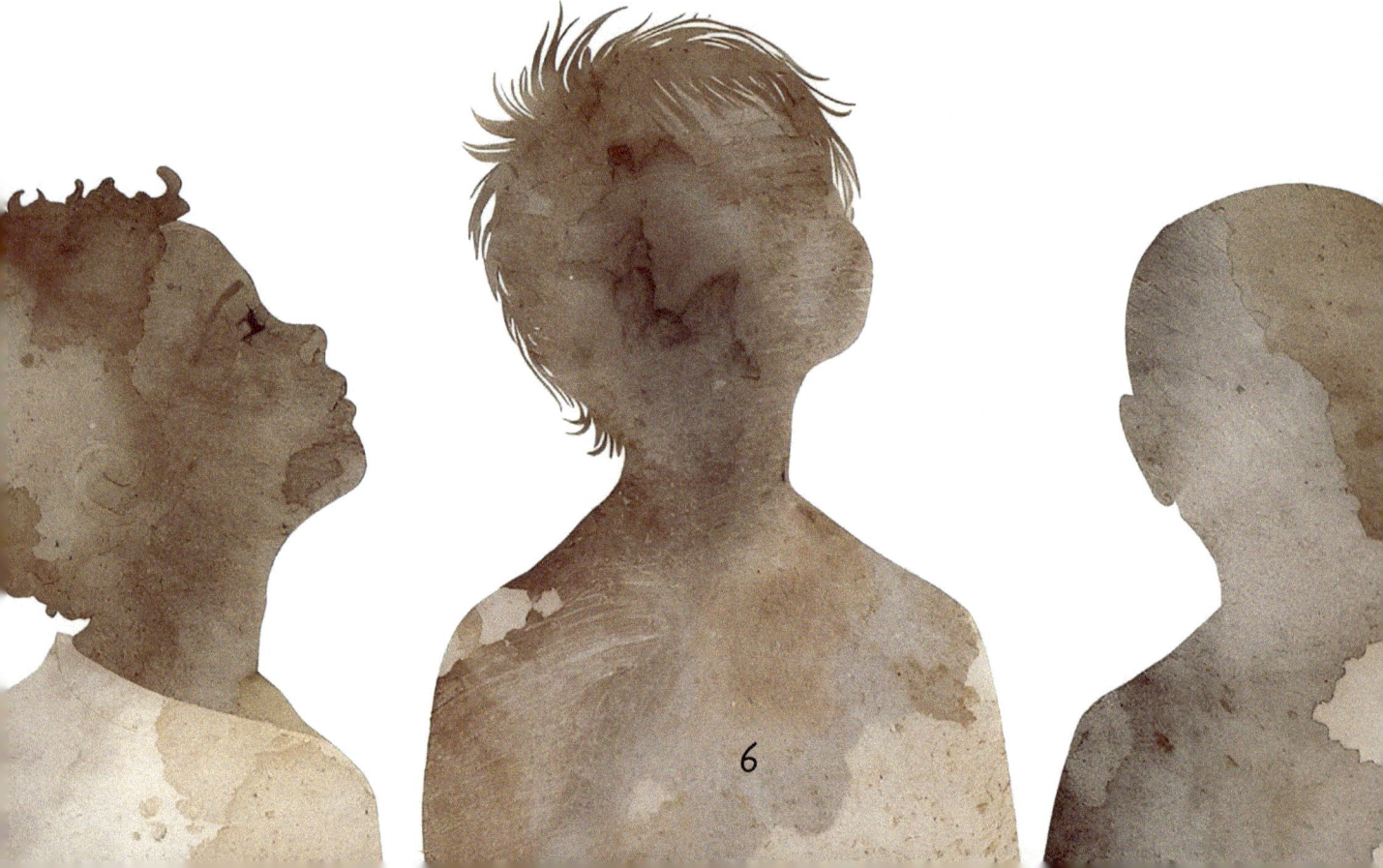

The 99 Names of Allah

- The All-Compassionate
- The All-Merciful
- The Absolute Ruler
- The Pure One
- The Source of Peace
- The Inspirer of Faith
- The Guardian
- The Victorious
- The Compeller
- The Greatest
- The Creator
- The Shaper of Beauty
- The Forgiving
- The Subduer
- The Giver of All
- The Sustainer
- The Opener
- The Knower of All
- The Constrictor
- The Reliever
- The Abaser
- The Exalter
- The Bestower of Honors
- The Humiliator
- The Hearer of All
- The Seer of All
- The Judge
- The Just
- The Subtle One
- The All-Aware
- The Forbearing
- The Magnificent
- The Forgiver and Hider of Faults
- The Rewarder of Thankfulness
- The Highest
- The Greatest
- The Preserver
- The Nourisher
- The Accounter
- The Mighty
- The Hidden One
- The Generous
- The Protecting Friend
- The Watchful One
- The Supreme One
- The Responder to Prayer
- The Perfectly Wise
- The Doer of Good
- The Loving One
- The Guide to Repentance
- The Majestic One
- The Avenger
- The Resurrector
- The Forgiver
- The Witness
- The Clement
- The Truth
- The Trustee
- The Owner of All
- The Governor
- The Lord of Majesty and Bounty
- The Forceful One
- The Gatherer
- The Equitable One
- The Praised One
- The Rich One
- The Appraiser
- The Enricher
- The Originator
- The Preventer of Harm
- The Restorer
- The Preventer of Harm
- The Creator of The Harmful
- The Creator of Good
- The Giver of Life
- The Taker of Life
- The Ever Living One
- The Light
- The Self-Existing One
- The Guide
- The Finder
- The Originator
- The Glorious
- The Everlasting One
- The Only One
- The One
- The Inheritor of All
- The Righteous Teacher
- The Satisfier of All Needs
- The Patient One
- The All Powerful
- The Creator of All Power
- The Expediter
- The Delayer
- The First
- The Last
- The Manifest One
- The Absolute Ruler

Christians pray, "Our Father in heaven, holy is Your name." (Matthew 6:9)

Jewish friends say, "Shema Yisrael, Adonai Eloheinu, Adonai Echad. Hear O Israel, the Lord our G-d, the Lord is One." (Deuteronomy 6:4)

Buddhists practice compassion through meditation,

Hindus honor the Supreme Spirit in daily rituals,

Native peoples speak to the Great Spirit
and live in harmony with nature.

Different ways to connect.
One Creator.

Prayer, meditation, and reflection
are like planting a seed in the heart.

They help people feel calm and focused.

They grow patience, kindness, and understanding.

Scientists have studied these practices and found they can improve health, reduce stress, and strengthen feelings of hope and connection.

The Prophet Abraham, peace be upon him,
is remembered as a friend of God.

From him came Judaism, Christianity, and Islam.
These religions are called The Abrahamic faiths.

Each faith has its own book:
the Torah, the Gospel (Bible), and the Qur'an.

Each teaches the same message:
there is only One Creator.
Love Him, serve Him,
and care for one another.

THE CALL TO WORSHIP

People are called to worship in many ways.

In Judaism, the shofar, a ram's horn, is blown to gather hearts in remembrance.
(Leviticus 23:24)

In Christianity, the church bell rings across towns to invite people to worship.
(Tradition rooted in Psalm 150:5 "Praise Him with the sounding of the trumpet")

In Islam, the human voice, the adhan, is raised to remind us that it is time to turn to Allah.
(Qur'an 62:9)

In Buddhism, the gentle gong or bell sounds to begin meditation and mindfulness.
(Dhammapada 1 — "All that we are is the result of what we have thought.")

In Hindu temples, conch shells and bells awaken devotion and signal the presence of the Divine.
(Bhagavata Purana 12.11.1 — conch and bell as sacred instruments)

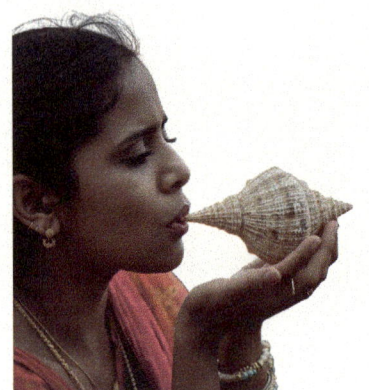

In Indigenous traditions, the steady drumbeat calls the community to honor the Great Spirit.
(Cherokee and Lakota oral traditions; drum called "the heartbeat of Mother Earth")

THOUSANDS OF PROPHETS

124,000 prophets and messengers
sent across time and cultures

And the line of prophets is long...

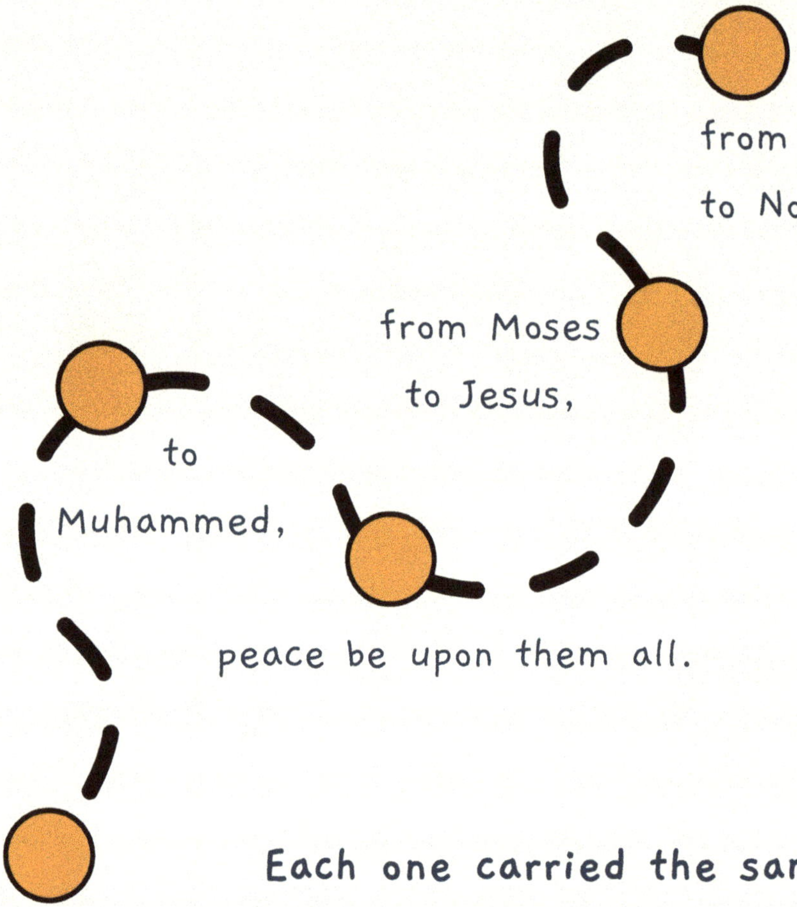

from Adam to Noah,

from Moses to Jesus,

to Muhammed,

peace be upon them all.

Each one carried the same light,
reminding us of the same Creator.

And there are other religions, too, that are gifts from The One.

Buddhists teach:
"Just as a mother would protect her only child with her life, even so let one cultivate a boundless love toward all beings.
Let one's thoughts of love pervade the whole world — above, below, and across — without obstruction, without hatred, without enmity."
(Pali Canon, Sutta Nipata 1.8)

Hindus say:
"The whole world is one family"
(Mahabharata, 5:1517)

Native peoples honor all life as connected through the Great Spirit.

Every path is a call toward the Highest.

People worship in many ways

Imams lead prayers in masajid (mosques).

Pastors guide church congregations.

Rabbis teach and lead Jewish communities.

Priests serve in temples or churches.

Monks and spiritual teachers meditate and teach wisdom.

Shamans and elders guide in connection with nature.

Like a garden with many flowers, our world is beautiful because it is full of variety.

The scriptures remind us to care for one another

The Qur'an: "O mankind! ... We made you into nations and tribes so that you may know one another..."
(Qur'an 49:11)

The Bible: "Love your neighbor as yourself."
(Mark 12:31)

The Torah: "You shall love the stranger, for you were strangers in the land of Egypt."
(Deuteronomy 10:19)

Hindu texts: "Be one to whom the guest is like God."
(Taittiriya Upanishad 1.11.2)

Buddhist teachings: "All beings fear harm; all beings love life. See yourself in others, and do not harm."
(Dhammapada 129-130)

Native traditions: "The Great Spirit is in all things: He is in the air we breathe. The Great Spirit is our Father, but the Earth is our Mother. She nourishes us; that which we put into the ground she returns to us."
(Big Thunder (Bedagi), Algonquin Elder)

Different words,
one message:
Be brothers and sisters in kindness.

We are remembering the same Creator.
The One who loves us all.

All around the world, people pray, sing,
meditate, bow, and give thanks.
Each in their own way,
but all to the One who created everything!

MANY WAYS TO WORSHIP
ONE CREATOR WHO HEARS THEM ALL

There are more than 4,000 religions in the world today.

That means there are billions of people who love, remember, and call upon the One Creator, using many beautiful names.

Islam
- Over 1.9 billion Muslims pray to Allah, five times a day, facing the Ka'bah in Makkah.
- They begin with "Bismillah" ("With the Name of G'd, the Merciful Benefactor, the Merciful Redeemer.")

Christianity
- Over 2.4 billion Christians worship God, whom they call "Our Father in Heaven."
- They pray, sing songs of praise, and gather in churches each week.

Judaism
- About 15 million Jews call on Adonai, saying the Shema: "Hear, O Israel, the Lord our G-d, the Lord is One."

Buddhism
- Around 500 million Buddhists practice mindfulness, meditation, and compassion, honoring the Divine spark in all living beings.

Hinduism
- Over 1.2 billion Hindus revere the Supreme Spirit, called Brahman, through prayer, chanting, and offerings of flowers and light.

Native and Indigenous Traditions
- Millions of Native peoples across the Americas and the world honor the Great Spirit, the Creator who gave life to all things.
- They show gratitude through songs, dance, and care for the Earth.

Though people have different languages, clothing, songs, and places of prayer, they are all reaching for the same Light, the same One who created the sun, moon, stars, and hearts that love.

Different paths. Different prayers.
One Creator, everywhere.

No need to argue about our differences and what divides us.

We are a part of one big creation and plan by One Masterful Designer.

May we find joy, peace, and goodness in honoring that Divine vision for humanity.

In the end, The One who created us will settle our differences. Until then, we can look for the beauty we share, celebrate our similarities, and build a world full of kindness, unity, and joy.

So let's remember:
Call on Allah,
or call on God,
or call on the Beneficent,
or call on The Almighty,
or call on the Great Spirit.

The name may change.
But the One we call on
is always the same.

And the most important thing...
is to call on Them.

One Creator.

One Light.

Many Names.

Activities & Reflections: Living the Message of "One Creator, Many Names"

1. Visit or Host: "A Day of Many Names"

Invite your school, masjid, church, synagogue, or community center to host an Interfaith Day of Understanding.

Option A: Visit Local Houses of Worship

Children and families can visit:
- A masjid to learn about the adhan (call to prayer).
- A church to hear the bells and prayers.
- A synagogue to see the Torah and learn the Shema.
- A temple to observe meditation, chanting, or rituals.
- An Indigenous center or nature space to learn how the Great Spirit is honored through harmony with creation.

Encourage children to listen respectfully, remove shoes or cover heads when appropriate, and ask thoughtful questions about what they observe.

Option B: Host an Interfaith Day at School or in Your Community
- Invite parents, clergy, or leaders (Imam, Pastor, Rabbi, Monk, Priest, Pandit, or Elder) to share one short prayer, reading, or song about peace.
- Create "Faith Stations" around the room — each with visuals (books, symbols, photos) and a short description of one belief tradition.
- Have children write or draw: "What do we all share?"
- End with a Unity Circle, where each child says one word about what connects us — love, peace, kindness, compassion, respect.

2. Classroom & Home Discussion Prompts

Teachers and parents can use these to deepen understanding:
- What do people mean when they say "One Creator"?
- What are some different names for the Creator in other faiths?
- Why do people pray, meditate, or pause? How does it help them feel connected?
- What do we all share when we show love, kindness, or respect?
- How can we honor people who pray or believe differently than we do?

3. Research & Reflection Projects

Encourage students to research or create projects such as:
- A "Prayer Around the World" collage — showing people praying or meditating in different cultures.
- A "Names of the Creator" poster — listing names from different faiths with translations and meanings.
- A Reflection Journal — children write about how they feel when they pray, meditate, or spend time in nature.
- A "Calls to Worship" sound project — collect recordings or videos of bells, shofars, adhans, drums, or chants.

4. Acts of Unity

Small actions children can take:
- Say a kind word or prayer for someone from another faith.
- Visit a neighbor's place of worship or invite them to yours.
- Help care for nature as an act of honoring the Creator's creation.
- Create an "Our World of Faiths" mural with drawings of sacred symbols, trees, and people from around the world.
- Explore how peace begins with each person choosing kindness instead of revenge.
- Activity idea: Create a "Circle of Compassion" — students draw or write names of people and beings they can send kind thoughts to.

Extra Discussion Prompts:
1. What are different ways people honor the Creator through nature and kindness?
2. Can you find ways your family's faith connects with the teachings of other faiths?
3. How do prayer, meditation, and quiet reflection help people in different religions?

Extra Activities:
- **Interfaith Prayer Circle:** Have children share a short prayer or blessing from any tradition.
- **Nature Journaling:** Draw and write about how caring for plants, water, or animals is a way to honor the Creator.
- **Faith Leader Match**: Match leaders (Imam, Rabbi, Pastor, Priest, Monk) to their faith community and learn a short greeting they use in prayer.
- **World Faith Map:** Create a classroom wall map showing where different faiths are practiced.
- **Art Project:** Draw how people around the world show love to God — through prayer, kindness, music, or caring for nature.

Bibliography & References

The Holy Qur'an   Translations by Abdullah Yusuf Ali, Muhammad Asad, and Saheeh International

The Holy Bible   Old and New Testaments, New International Version (NIV), King James Version (KJV)

The Torah   Deuteronomy 6:4 "Shema Yisrael, Adonai Eloheinu, Adonai Echad"

The Bhagavad Gita   Verses on Divine Unity and Duty (Chapters 4 and 9), translation by Eknath Easwaran

The Dhammapada (Buddhist Teachings)   Verses on Loving-Kindness and Compassion (Chapters 1, 5, and 15)

Native American Wisdom Texts   Lakota Sacred Teachings and The Great Spirit and the Circle of Life (Oral traditions, various nations)

40 Hadith Sayings of the Prophet Muhammad (peace be upon him)

Continue the Journey

These books continue the message of unity, peace, and understanding found in One Creator, Many Names. We share the following books as an invitation for children, families, and classrooms to explore the world's faiths, celebrate our shared humanity, and discover the many ways people around the globe honor the One Creator.
May each story and guide encourage curiosity, compassion, and joy in learning about the beautiful diversity of our human family.

Children's Books

- Golden Domes and Silver Lanterns: A Muslim Book of Colors by Hena Khan
    A beautifully illustrated introduction to Islamic faith and culture through color and poetry.
- One World, Many Faiths by Karen Armstrong
    A gentle, illustrated journey through the world's major religions, written by a world-renowned scholar.
- Many Ways: How Families Practice Their Beliefs and Religions Around the World by Shelly Rotner and Sheila M. Kelly
    Real photographs show how families around the world pray, celebrate, and show kindness.
- What Do You Believe? by DK Publishing
    A visual guide for children that explains the world's faith traditions side by side, emphasizing similarities.
- Faith: Five Religions and What They Share by Dr. Diane Levert
    A simple yet profound exploration of Judaism, Christianity, Islam, Hinduism, and Buddhism.
- A World of Faith by Peggy Fletcher Stack, illustrated by Kathleen B. Peterson
    An inclusive introduction to different religions through stories and symbols.

- Same, Same but Different by Jenny Sue Kostecki-Shaw
    - A charming story about friendship across cultures and continents, teaching unity through difference.
- God's Dream by Archbishop Desmond Tutu and Douglas Carlton Abrams
    - A warm, faith-filled picture book about forgiveness, love, and seeing one another as part of God's dream.
- Children Just Like Me: Celebrations! by DK and UNICEF
    - A look at how children around the world honor life, faith, and community through special traditions.
- In God's Name by Rabbi Sandy Eisenberg Sasso
    - Introduces children to the many names by which God is known across different cultures and religions. It's a poetic exploration of the divine from various faith perspectives.
- What Is God's Name? by Rabbi Sandy Eisenberg Sasso
    - An adaptation for younger children, this book helps them understand the different ways people personify God and why.
- A Children's Treasury of Prayers by L. Bleck
    - An anthology that includes prayers from many cultures and faiths, speaking directly to children's concerns and understanding.
- You Be You by Linda Kranz
    - Through the story of Adri, a little fish exploring the ocean, this book promotes interfaith understanding by highlighting the beauty of diversity that exists in the world.

For Parents, Educators, and Older Readers
- The World's Religions by Huston Smith
    A timeless overview of major faith traditions with deep respect for each path.
- The Faith Club: A Muslim, A Christian, A Jew—Three Women Search for Understanding by Ranya Idliby, Suzanne Oliver, and Priscilla Warner
    An inspiring model of interfaith friendship and dialogue.
- Religions of the World by Elizabeth Breuilly, Joanne O'Brien, and Martin Palmer
    An illustrated resource on world religions, rituals, and the values they share.
- Kindness: The Little Thing That Matters Most by Jaime Thurston
    A heart-centered guide for fostering empathy and love across differences.

About the author

Qur'an Shakir aka Madame Q was born and raised Muslim in the United States and has dedicated over 40 years to interfaith work, building understanding and connections among diverse communities. She is passionate about educating children and families about the shared values of faith, kindness, and respect for all creation. Through her writing, Qur'an Shakir creates thoughtful, inclusive stories that celebrate the unity of humanity and the beauty of diversity in belief, practice, and culture. She is a mother, grandmother, a master educator, author, and visionary editor with over four decades of experience in teaching, leadership, and curriculum development.

About B.U.B.I. (Building Us Beyond Imagination) Publishing

B.U.B.I. Publishing (Building Us Beyond Imagination Publishing) is a mission-driven publishing company founded by Qur'an Shakir, affectionately known as Madame Q, who says she name the publishing company B.U.B.I. as an acronym for Building Us Beyond Imagination, and as a tribute to her ancestors who were stolen from this island hundreds of years ago, and brought to the Americas as enslaved Africans.

B.U.B.I. Publishing is dedicated to uplifting the voices of children who write, teachers who write, and aspiring authors with a passion for storytelling that heals, inspires, and builds strong communities.

Our focus is on literature that celebrates creation and the Creator, encourages healing and self-love, and supports mental, emotional, and spiritual well-being. Through children's books, educational works, and empowering stories, we strive to nurture a healthier, stronger sense of family and community. At B.U.B.I. Publishing, we believe in the power of words to help us grow beyond imagination—into our best, most authentic selves.

"Thank you www.africanancestry.com for helping our family to discover that we are from the Bubi Tribe on the Bioko Island, an island near Equitorial Guinea, West Africa."

www.ingramcontent.com/pod-product-compliance
Lightning Source LLC
Chambersburg PA
CBHW062024050526
44107CB00105B/869